youthwriterscamp.com

Greetings to All!

Welcome to those who have decided to give this young author's first book a read. We believe in youth and their stories so much that we believe we can be a part of helping them tell their stories. We have been so inspired to see them grow and change.

Our Youth Writers Camp provides continuous opportunities for healthy emotional expression within a safe and supportive community. Our goal is to both to help young people cope through writing and to motivate them to develop their own streams of revenue.

Brandon C Allen, LLC is actively engaging today's youth with an aim to increase mental and emotional health outcomes. However, we understand that our efforts to positively impact the mental and emotional health of this current generation won't reach maximum effectiveness unless we have the support of the entire community.

THIS IS WHERE YOU COME IN.

Through the things they discovered about themselves, the lessons about mental health, and the coping techniques they garnered during this time, it is our job as a community to continue to cultivate their development and empower them to shift their own realities into the best versions designed for them. Our hope is that these students feel loved, cared for, and equipped enough to continue to heal and process with healthy coping tools and creative avenues. Thank you for investing in this student, one poem at a time.

Students, congratulations and I am proud of all you accomplished. Continue to be all you are meant to be.

Brandon Allen, Author and Founder of Youth Writers Camp

Dear Rayjuan,

Do you know what you just did? Seriously. Think about it. You wrote your first book. Did you know that a recent survey of 2,000 U.S. respondents reveals just 15 percent have started writing a book, and a mere six percent have gotten halfway through?

You beat the odds. Many say what they are going to do. Some start it, then abandon it—very few finish. You finished.

Growing up, I always kept a journal. Writing and playing the piano were my first loves. Had I known of a program like this and had a teacher like Brandon Allen, I would have been an author at seven years old. Serving alongside Brandon and making many young authors' dreams come true is a blessing.

Remember, this is just your first step in a long and adventurous journey. Always write. Writing can serve as a constant and reliable best friend.

With love and poetry,

Camari Carter Hawkins
Author and Founder of Mama's Kitchen Press

A RAY OF LIGHT'S SHADOW

Rayjuan Horton

MAMA'S KITCHEN PRESS

A Ray of Light's Shadow
©2023 Rayjuan Horton
ISBN: 979-8-9893829-1-0

First Edition, 2023

Printed in the United States of America

Cover & Layout Design by Emily Anne Evans

*I want to dedicate this book to my uncles,
Alexander James and Aaron Miranda.*

*Thanks for encouraging me and providing
me with words of wisdom.*

Contents

Foreword

A Ray of Light's Shadow is a wonderful assortment of a young man's point of view of his life, his learning and relationships. Being his mother I might have some partiality, but I'm proud of his growth that can be seen in each of the pieces presented. The lucidity of context adds character, marked by time that many readers can relate to.

Thank you for taking the time to read my son's poetry. I hope you enjoy this collection as much as I do.

Sharon Johnson

A RAY
OF LIGHT'S
SHADOW

Unknown Hero

Rayuno, Raynito, Rayjon, Rawr-J,
Ray-Ray, Rayjunior, Ray, and RJ
So many names he goes by.
Which one is it? Well if I told you, would it truly be the truth or
a lie?

Relying on the power of Christ, his joyful spirit shines like the
stars.
His speed is unmatched, yet his empathy is probably his
strongest ability.
And his poetic nature also comes in handy.
For this hero's goal is to help humanity.

Yet every hero has their weaknesses, the lack of strength that holds them back.
He's not that strong, avoids confrontation, and doesn't like to attack.
Believing words can truly reach the heart, he's like a psychiatrist with the right prescription.
Though many may revolt against him, his goal remains pure.

He doesn't do early morning interviews, but late night talk shows.
But this is all we know about our hero with many names.
Now shining bright, the brightest star you'll see tonight.
This is Rayjuan Horton signing off until next time.

The Masking Dead Days

It was a nice day.
Everything was good and okay.
It was finally spring.
The season with buzzing bees and the time allergies sing.

At the time I could hear the laughter of my friends.
But soon, I would never hear them again.
Now we have school behind a screen,
Due to the zombies outside lurking.

Now I was trapped inside of my house.
I knew it like the back of my hand.
The bright days never matched the chaos that ensued.
Talking to zombies was something brand new.

Masks stopped conversations.
Personal space was finally a thing.
It was a great time
For those who were antisocial and introverted to shine.

I was shining like a star.
But I was also a zombie.
My siblings avoided me like the plague.
Then my mother was soon infected.

I don't want to go back to those days.
Though I won't lie, I enjoyed the space.
Now I'm with my friends.
Now I can hear their laughter again.

Stomach Problems

Donuts are sweet circular desserts,
But how can this sweet treat hurt?
That pink frosting now a bright red.
Flaming sprinkles, so, and it just spreads.

It's so spicy but my face wouldn't show it,
A loop of anger is my stomach, and the burning is legit.
But there is also the frosty cold treat.
It's ice cream, a delightful treat.

Eating it makes everything freeze,
Yet the tears don't.
Even if it's one pint,
I just want to be alone tonight.

An Easier Friendship

Why do I have to be into
What you are into
So we can start this friendship?
Why do I have to be into
What you are into?

Do I have to change me,
My personality,
And my view on reality
To fix your view
Of me in your mind?

Why do I have to be into
What you are into
So we can form this special bond?
Why do I have to be into
What you are into?

Is not friendship-building about
You and me
And adapting to each other's personalities?
So maybe then
I wouldn't have to ask the same question again.

Cause I want to change for
God, me, and people who truly believe in me.
Not to fit into the way you think of me.
So I will stay strong
Through all trials and tribulations.

So why do I have to be into
What you are into?
Could it be
Can it possibly
Make friendship easier.

Tell Me, My Friend

I give you my hand,
I just want to get closer to you.
I wanted to help with any of your crazy issues,
But I couldn't help and that's my greatest fear.

If I were to know everything about you,
But I could never ever help you,
It would kill me inside
That I wasn't enough for you.

So tell me, tell me, tell me, my friend.
I want to hear your problems, fears, and troubles, my friend.
And know that I'm here for you always and forever,
Cause all I want to do is help and make you happy.

So tell me, tell me, tell me, my friend.
Am I doing enough or am I overwhelming you with all my love?
Has my greatest fear come true,
Was I not able to help you?

I know it worries you that I worry about you,
And sometimes that worries me too.
And I just really want to know
If I make you happy at all.

But inside I know this fear is not real or right.
I cannot read your mind.
So I will just trust in you,
And hopefully everything turns out fine and true.

Cupid's Such a People Pleaser

I held cupid's bow for a minute.
Who could have guessed the tragedies about to unfold?
But how could these events be foretold?
Yet at that moment, I was in it to win it.

With those whose emotions were out of hand,
Thinking I could understand it all.
I tried to help and make it better but my efforts were too small.
I guess sometimes love is not the answer, other times it was a
demand.

I lost my identity with every arrow shot, like killing a pure
white dove.
Giving my heart to the world with a smile, never realizing
what I lost.
Then He appeared, returning my heart to me, and paying the
cost.
I was called to the Heavens, for I had forgotten the true
definition of love.

Then I realized cupid is not for me, such a teaser.
I let go of that bow,
Finally able to see real love, how it shines and glows.
Cupid's such a people pleaser.

Now I can see the light
And the warmth of real love.
No longer pushed and shoved,
Now in the hands of God who has all the love and it feels right.

Now I hold a pen writing about all the ways He's good to me,
Even in my poetry.
And unlike a people pleaser, I was in no hurry.
Now I'm finally free.

Looking back I can see that I've matured.
I'm glad to not be the person that I used to be,
And I'm pretty sure God agrees.
Now I'm in the Kingdom where real love thrives and I'm
secured.

Carousel Camaraderie

Round and round we go,
An endless rotation that we only know.
Walking around the gate of noble steeds,
Yet every time we turn the corner,
We only catch a glimpse of each other.

Why walk if we only get farther?
Why run if we can't get any closer?
I almost gave up.
Now I wait at the gate,
Looking at the horses glimmering in the light.

Almost blinded,
Now you standing next to me
At the Carousel of Camaraderie.
Now will you ride with me
On this merry go round of friendship?

Childish Wish

My wish, my wish
To make you the perfect dish.
One that'll make you laugh and smile
For a long, long while.

A dish that is sweet and cool,
And beautiful like you.
I wish you always to be safe and sheltered.
Always in the hands of God.

Know that I love you,
And without you, we wouldn't know what to do.
The wish for you, first child:
That you have lots of fun and always smile.

Hopeful Shine

I don't see it in you.
I don't believe it's true.
How would you ever make it?

All the small comments,
All so hopeless.
Maybe it's true, you can't do it.

No, those are lies.
Anyone can say anything,
But it's up to you if you want to change things.

You shouldn't let the world define you.
But don't close the door on those who truly love you
Because it's those hopeful words.

They'll help you rise.
Knowing that someone wants the best for you will make you
shine
Like me, I got the Lord at my side.

The world is so full of deception,
But listen now to this important lesson.
It's up to you if you're going to listen to all those lies.

It's up to you if you're going to sin tonight.
It's up to you because you're the only one who lets the
darkness in.
So get up, get out there, and shine.

Because it is time for you to replace those lies with the truth.
And for those who believe in Jesus Christ our Lord and Savior,
Philippians 4:13 should work in your favor.

Hear This Voice

This voice given to me is like a small ball of light.
Why is it so small and dim?
Could it ever be a big, flaming ball of light?

If I keep it to myself it won't grow,
If I give it back to Him it will surely thrive.
With it, my confidence will grow.

I reach for vocal confidence, confidence in my voice.
God, I give it to you,
So when I praise your name you hear my voice.

About the Author

Rayjuan Horton just started High School in Orange County, California. He has been writing poems since the 7th grade. Youth Writers Camp has helped him explore his emotions more through poetry. *A Ray of Light's Shadow* is a book about how your emotions are there, but they aren't you. He hopes you have an amazing time reading it.